INTRODUCTION

Did you know that there are more than 300 named and nameless women mentioned in the Bible? But who is counting? What matters is that the women count; they are invaluable to our salvation history. From Eve to the Bride, God's saving love is manifested through women. Just as women play sometimes subtle yet always significant roles in the Scriptures, they continue to do so in our lives today.

I invite you to meet some of the women of the Bible noted in these prayers. You may want to begin your day by reading one of these reflections and praying for the women in today's society of whom the passage speaks. You may even find yourself called to name and pray for specific women in your life. As we offer up the needs of countless women, may we be assured that, although our society does not always value their worth, our God surely treasures all women.

18 Powerful Women of the Bible

Scripture Passages,
Reflections &
Compassionate Prayers

SARAH THOMAS TRACY

TWENTY-THIRD PUBLICATIONS
twentythirdpublications.com

Twenty-Third Publications
977 Hartford Turnpike Unit A
Waterford, CT 06385
(860) 437-3012 or (800) 321-0411
www.twentythirdpublications.com

Copyright © 2023 Twenty-Third Publications. All rights reserved. No part of this publication may be reproduced in any manner without prior written permission of the publisher. Write to the Permissions Editor.

The Scripture passages contained herein are from the New Revised Standard Version Bible, Catholic edition. Copyright ©1989, by the Division of Christian Education of the National Council of the Churches of Christ in the U.S.A. All rights reserved.

ISBN: 978-1-62785-746-8
Printed in the U.S.A.

bayard A division of Bayard, Inc.

Part 1

UNNAMED WOMEN

LET'S COUNT THE WOMEN

The Women Present in the Crowd

Taking the five loaves and the two fish, he looked up to heaven, and blessed and broke the loaves, and gave them to the disciples, and the disciples gave them to the crowds. And all ate and were filled...And those who ate were about five thousand men, besides women and children. MATTHEW 14:19-21

PAUSE & REFLECT
There are a few miracles in this gospel passage known as the multiplication of the loaves and fishes. The obvious one is that five loaves of bread and two fish fed a crowd of at least five thousand men—not counting women and children—to the point of satisfaction. And there were leftovers! Another miracle may be that as the baskets of food were passed among the crowd, people shared what little they may have had with them, adding to the bounty. A third, striking miracle is that no one went away hungry. The five thousand men and uncounted women and children ate and were satisfied.

HEAR OUR PRAYER...
Jesus, our Bread of Life, today there are multitudes who suffer from starvation and food insecurity. We pray especially for single mothers: women who comfort their malnourished children, women who ignore their own hunger pangs and weakness to feed their children with what little they have. May the miracle of sharing our gifts and resources with our sisters and brothers take root so that all will be fed to the point of satisfaction. Amen.

LET'S SHARE OUR TREASURES

The Poor Widow

He looked up and saw rich people putting their gifts into the treasury; he also saw a poor widow put in two small copper coins. He said, "Truly I tell you, this poor widow has put in more than all of them; for all of them have contributed out of their abundance, but she out of her poverty has put in all she had to live on." LUKE 21:1-4

PAUSE & REFLECT

Most of the widows we meet in the Bible are recipients, not givers. They are subjects of compassion, mercy, even pity. Widows are dependent upon others for their survival. The widow whom Jesus meets—a woman who is poor herself—is a giver. And for that reason, she makes many of us uncomfortable. She does not give of her excess; she gives from her own need. Unlike most people, she offers what she cannot spare. We may say, "I have an extra $20 bill in my wallet. I'll put that in the donation box. Here's that old winter coat that I haven't worn in years. I'll bring it to the Red Cross bin. I have more cans of soup in my cupboard than I can eat. I'll bring a couple of the extra ones to the food pantry." Seldom do we donate our last $20, our single winter coat, or the only food we have left. We tend to donate from our abundance.

HEAR OUR PRAYER...

We pray for the women in our cities and neighborhoods who sleep in shelters, dine in soup kitchens, and shop at food pantries. Like the widow in the Bible, these women make us uncomfortable: we fear that we, too, may suffer from the injustices of poverty. And so, we make ourselves feel better by giving to them. Yet, we are challenged to give of our treasure—not solely our earthly treasure. We thank the "poor widows" of today who remind us that we are called to dig deep into our hearts, to empty ourselves of all that God has given us: compassion, kindness, respect, love. Amen.

LET'S WELCOME ALL OF GOD'S CHILDREN

The Samaritan Woman

The Samaritan woman said to him, "How is it that you, a Jew, ask a drink of me, a woman of Samaria?" (Jews do not share things in common with Samaritans.) Jesus answered her, "If you knew the gift of God, and who it is that is saying to you, 'Give me a drink,' you would have asked him, and he would have given you living water."
JOHN 4:9-10

PAUSE & REFLECT
This woman from Samaria has a questionable lifestyle: she has had five husbands and she is not married to her current partner. She is an outcast in her village. She approaches the well at noon, when the other women have already drawn their water at a cooler time of day and returned home, so she would not have to hear their insults or see their judging glances. To her dismay, she is not alone at the well. There is a man there: a Jewish man who dares to break the law and speak to her, a Samaritan. He is gentle and kind; he knows of her past and

her lifestyle and yet he is tender and accepting. He does not condemn her; no, he blesses her by revealing himself as the Christ. She is freed from shame.

HEAR OUR PRAYER...
We pray for mothers who struggle with their children's gender identity and sexual orientation. Mothers whose children suffer from the isolation, condemnation, and insults that the Samaritan woman endured. Women who love their children so deeply and who always will love them, no matter what. Yet, these women find themselves conflicted when faced with Church doctrine. May these women and their children meet the tender, accepting Jesus at the well and drink of his life-giving water. While others judge and isolate, we pray that these mothers and their LGBTQ+ children will experience Jesus' embracing, inclusive love through their neighbors, fellow parishioners, coworkers, and loved ones. In the words of Pope Francis to parents of LGBTQ+ individuals, "God loves your children as they are because they are the children of God." Amen.

LET'S FREE THE IMPRISONED

The Penitent Woman

One of the Pharisees asked Jesus to eat with him, and he went into the Pharisee's house ... And a woman in the city who was a sinner, having learned that he was eating in the Pharisee's house, brought an alabaster jar of ointment. She stood behind him at his feet, weeping, and began to bathe his feet with her tears and to dry them with her hair... kissing his feet and anointing them with the ointment. LUKE 7:36-38

PAUSE & REFLECT
This woman who bathes and anoints Jesus' feet has a shameful reputation. The self-righteous Pharisee looks upon her with disdain. He sees only her immorality and transgressions and is blind to his own sinfulness. The Penitent Woman has her own personal story, unknown to others; she has her own reasons that brought about her wrongdoings. But that was all in her past now. In this encounter with Jesus, she is a woman who acknowledges her sins but does not allow them to define her. This woman's desire for forgiveness and healing dared her to join the Pharisee's dinner party; she was an uninvited guest who knew Jesus in a way that the host did not understand. The Penitent Woman's adoration and unspoken request for forgiveness exposes Jesus' healing compassion. While the other guests and the host looked upon her with disgust and questioned Jesus' response to her, the Penitent Woman was set free.

HEAR OUR PRAYER...
We pray, with the Penitent Woman, for all women throughout our world who are imprisoned. Like the Pharisee, seldom do we look within these women to see who they are; more often, we see only the actions they have been accused of doing. Their stories remain untold. They were once children, young girls with hopes and dreams. We do not know the trauma, the violence done to them that may have brought them to these

prison walls. May these women encounter the healing compassion of Jesus and may his forgiveness set them free. Amen.

LET'S GRIEVE OUR CHILDREN

The Shunammite Woman

When the child was older, he went out one day to his father among the reapers. He complained to his father, "Oh, my head, my head!" The father said to his servant, "Carry him to his mother." He carried him and brought him to his mother; the child sat on her lap until noon, and he died. 2 KINGS 4:18-20

PAUSE & REFLECT

It is an ordinary day in the life of the Shunammite woman and her family. Her beloved long-awaited son had grown in years and stature and was now old enough to work in the fields with his father. She watched him walk off to join his father's side, wondering where the years had gone and dreaming of where the future would take her son. But how quickly things changed. The quiet normalcy that was taken for granted was shattered. The boy now lies lifeless in his mother's lap. The Shunammite woman is overcome with grief and shock; she reacts as all mothers do: This cannot be! I will not let my son die! I will find help! I will demand that my child's life be restored!

HEAR OUR PRAYER...
There are mothers today, at this very moment, who hold their child's lifeless bodies in their arms. Violence, illness, and accidents bring mothers to their knees, crying out, "This cannot be!" We pray for mothers whose children have died. Regardless of the child's age, a mother is shattered by her child's death. Whether the cause is a lengthy illness or a sudden accident, a mother is never prepared for her child's death. We pray for all mothers who have lost a child; women who continue to live with a void that will always remain. Just as the Shunammite woman ran to the holy man Elisha to heal her son, we pray that today's grieving mothers turn to you, Jesus, with hope and faith that their children have been gathered to your side, brought back to life, and now share in the newness of eternal life. Amen.

LET'S RAISE OUR VOICES

The Canaanite Woman

The woman came and knelt before him. "Lord, help me!" she said. He replied, "It is not right to take the children's bread and toss it to the dogs." "Yes, it is, Lord," she said. "Even the dogs eat the crumbs that fall from their master's table." Then Jesus said to her, "Woman, you have great faith! Your request is granted." **MATTHEW 15:25-28**

PAUSE & REFLECT

This Gentile woman from Cana has three strikes against her: her religion was wrong, her gender was wrong, and her nationality was wrong. But she spoke up and she spoke out. Initially, she requested that Jesus heal her daughter—a desperate plea made to this holy Jewish man by a Gentile woman. But Jesus rebuffs her; at this point in his ministry, his focus is on the Israelites. Yet, the Canaanite Woman is persistent, and her reply to Jesus is clever. She speaks the truth of justice. She will not take no for an answer. The woman risked that her request would be rejected by Jesus a second time. It was a risk she was willing to take for more than her daughter's healing; she was making an appeal for a greater healing—that the injustices and prejudices she encounters be eliminated.

HEAR OUR PRAYER...

We pray for all women who speak up and speak out, women whose voices call us to name the injustices that exist in our societies and to right them. We see these women rally at our government offices, march in our streets, and peacefully protest in our cities. Like the Canaanite Woman, they take risks and are persistent in their call for healing our societal wrongs: they call for fair wages, racial and gender equality, and an end to all types of violence. May their voices change our hearts and deepen our love for all as the voice of the Canaanite woman changed Jesus' heart. Amen.

LET'S BLESS OUR EARTH

"Naamah," Noah's Wife

But I will establish my covenant with you, and you shall come into the ark, you, your sons, your wife, and your sons' wives with you. And of every living thing, of all flesh, you shall bring two of every kind into the ark, to keep them alive with you; they shall be male and female.
GENESIS 6:18-19

PAUSE & REFLECT
God did not appoint Noah alone to provide for the animals during the great flood. It was a responsibility shared among his family. And so, Noah's wife also cared for the animals, keeping them alive as God commanded. Though she is unnamed in the Bible, both Jewish and Catholic tradition give Noah's wife the name "Naamah." Jewish legend explains that she is given this name because her deeds were *neimen*—pleasing. And what were her deeds? A children's book titled *A Prayer for the Earth: The Story of Naamah, Noah's Wife*, by Sandy Eisenberg Sasso, tells the story that God called upon Naamah to save the plants of the earth. She gathers the seeds of every type of plant, then sows the seeds and tends to the seedlings. Regardless of Noah's wife's name, and aside from the fictional story of her saving the plants, the Bible tells us that she played a role in gathering the animals into the ark, caring for them during the flood, and keeping them alive, so that once the waters had receded, the animals were brought out of the ark so they could "abound on the earth, and be fruitful and multiply" on it (Genesis 8:17).

HEAR OUR PRAYER...
We pray for all women who are stewards of our earth, who care for our environment, and who preserve our natural places. We pray for women who educate us on environmental concerns: women whose professions save and protect our planet. We pray for women whose practices of recycling, conservation, gardening, and minimalism promote our earth's health. We pray for all women who pause through their daily life to admire and appreciate and offer thanks for the beauty of God's creation. Amen.

LET'S PRAY TOGETHER

The Daughter of Jairus

Then one of the leaders of the synagogue named Jairus came and, when he saw [Jesus], fell at his feet and begged him repeatedly, "My little daughter is at the point of death. Come and lay your hands on her, so that she may be made well, and live." MARK 5:22-23

PAUSE & REFLECT
The daughter of Jairus, a 12-year-old girl, is so sick that she is at the point of death. Her desperate father leaves his daughter's bedside and seeks out healing—not from a physician but from Jesus. Jairus had heard of Jesus' healing power, and he knew and believed that if Jesus laid his hands on the girl, she would be made well and would live. We do not know any of the details; we do not know the girl's name, what illness she had, or how long she had been sick. We do know that she relied

on the faith of her father to seek out Jesus and to request that Jesus heal her. Of course, the girl herself wanted to be cured; she relied on her father's intercession so she might live.

HEAR OUR PRAYER...
We pray for all the women—young or old—who have asked us to pray for them. Women who know of our faith and trust in Jesus and who have requested that we bring their needs to the Father. We pray for women who desire physical cures and emotional healing. We pray for women who ask that their families be reunited. We pray for women who struggle financially. We pray for all women who rely upon us, as the daughter of Jairus relied upon her father, to intercede for them and to bring their needs to our Father. May we plead repeatedly for their needs. Amen.

LET'S PLACE ANOTHER FIRST

The True Mother

The other woman said, "No, the living son is mine, and the dead son is yours." The first said, "No, the dead son is yours, and the living son is mine."...The king said, "One says, 'This is my son that is alive, and your son is dead'; while the other says, 'Not so! Your son is dead, and my son is the living one.'" So the king said, "Bring me a sword ... Divide the living boy in two; then give half to one, and half to the other." But the woman whose son was alive said to the king—because compassion for her son burned within her—"Please, my lord, give her the living boy; certainly do not kill him!" 1 KINGS 3:22-26

Pause & Reflect

King Solomon is called upon to resolve a dispute between two mothers, both of whom are claiming that the living baby boy is theirs. While Solomon's suggested resolution to the situation and his later judgment reveal his God-given gift of wisdom (a gift that he had just asked of God), it also depicts the depth of a mother's love for her child. The real mother would go to any lengths to save her child; she offers her son to the other woman to save his life; whereas the other woman's selfish desire for vengeance overpowered her love for the child. It is difficult to imagine that any woman would agree to Solomon's order to cut the child in half; however, the true mother's willingness to surrender her child to another so that he may live is understandable.

Hear Our Prayer...

We pray for women who, like the actual mother in this passage, deny themselves for the safety of another. We pray for women who live in war-torn countries; for teachers who actively interfere with school intruders; for female police officers, firefighters, and military personnel who risk their lives daily. We pray for all women who sacrifice their desires, their physical and emotional needs, their safety for the welfare of another. Amen.

Part II

Named Women

LET'S SPEAK THE TRUTH

Anna

There was also a prophet, Anna the daughter of Phanuel, of the tribe of Asher. She was of a great age, having lived with her husband for seven years after her marriage, then as a widow to the age of eighty-four. She never left the temple but worshiped there with fasting and prayer night and day. At that moment she came, and began to praise God and to speak about the child to all who were looking for the redemption of Jerusalem. LUKE 2:36-38

PAUSE & REFLECT

Anna, the prophetess of God: an elderly woman who lived many years alone as a widow. A woman who gained strength, knowledge, and confidence through the years. A woman of deep faith who knew the Hebrew Scriptures and who had the prophetic wisdom to recognize the Christ Child. Anna, a woman of grace and intuition. Anna, your age gained you a place in society; your slow gait, wrinkled complexion, and gray hair personified your wisdom.

Our world recently suffered the horrors of a pandemic: over six million people have died; jobs have been lost; children have missed valuable classroom time. But something else happened in the modern world: lockdowns kept women from hair salons and spas. Women have allowed their visible signs of aging to be revealed. Our graying hair and wrinkles around our eyes are noticeable.

HEAR OUR PRAYER...
We pray to you, Anna the Prophetess: may women who are advanced in years embrace the truth of who they are, acknowledging the wisdom they have gained through the years. Like Anna, we, too, are women of grace and intuition. Our years give us the self-confidence to speak the truth that lives in our hearts. Like Anna, we recognize the Christ in our midst while others' eyes are closed. We pray that we will follow you, our sister Anna, and challenge the false whisperings that echo in our world by speaking aloud the truth. May our world hear and ponder the prophetic wisdom of our wise, experienced women. Amen.

LET'S THANK OUR FRIENDS

Ruth and Naomi

So [Naomi] said, "See, your sister-in-law has gone back to her people and to her gods; return after your sister-in-law." But Ruth said, "Do not press me to leave you or to turn back from following you! Where you go, I will go; where you lodge, I will lodge; your people shall be my people, and your God my God. Where you die, I will die—there will I be buried. May the Lord do thus and so to me, and more as well, if even death parts me from you!" RUTH 1:15-18

PAUSE & REFLECT
This passage that retells the conversation between Ruth (derived from the Hebrew word *re'ut*, meaning "friend"), and her mother-in-law, Naomi (meaning "pleasantness"), is often

read at wedding ceremonies. Ruth's selfless promise to walk through life with Naomi and Naomi's God is a vow full of hope, love, and loyalty. The relationship between Ruth and Naomi personifies God's loving kindness. These two women embody God's call to practice *hesed*: steadfast love. While there are many differences between Naomi and Ruth—age, religion, culture—their tragic losses unite them. Above all, their love transcends all differences.

HEAR OUR PRAYER...
We pray with gratitude for our women friends, for our "Ruths." We may experience loving and being loved by a spouse, our children, parents, or siblings, but a friendship between women is a unique bond. The gift of a woman friend, while not rare, is to be cherished. A woman friend is a mirror, reflecting back to us our own strengths, joys, tears, and hopes. A woman friend shows us how to love ourselves as she loves us. Above all, a woman friend shows us how to love ourselves as God loves us. In her 1995 book *She Who Dwells Within*, Rabbi Lynn Gottlieb wrote about Ruth and Naomi's friendship: "God in this story does not reveal himself from a bush or a mountain or a dream or direct speech. Rather the presence of God is manifest through the love and caring of one woman for another."

Thank you, Lord, for those women who bring your loving kindness and steadfast love to my life. Amen.

LET'S BEAR GOD'S WORD

Sarah

God said to Abraham, "As for Sarai your wife, you shall not call her Sarai, but Sarah shall be her name. I will bless her, and moreover I will give you a son by her. I will bless her, and she shall give rise to nations; kings of peoples shall come from her." GENESIS 17:15-16

PAUSE & REFLECT

By God's command, Sarai the Princess becomes Sarah the Chieftainess. She is divinely selected as the mother of God's Chosen People. While Sarah is most well-known for the miraculous birth of her son, Isaac, at the advanced age of 90 years, she is to be recognized for her divinely ordained ministry as a spiritual guide of the women. Sarah was a woman of an array of emotions that she readily expressed: joy, skepticism, jealousy, anger, and laughter. Perhaps it is because of her humanness that women listened to her, followed her example, and came to know the God of Sarah and Abraham. Sarah set the stage for God's miraculous way of making what seems impossible possible through women. God's promise to Abraham of many descendants was fulfilled through the elderly and barren Sarah. Sarah's daughter-in-law Rebecca facilitated Isaac's birthright to be passed on to their second-born son, Jacob, not the firstborn Esau, as tradition demanded. Centuries later, another aged, barren woman is with child: Elizabeth gives birth to John the Baptist. And the greatest of all impossibilities becomes real: a young virgin, Mary, delivered the Messiah into the world.

HEAR OUR PRAYER...
We pray for those women whom God has chosen to turn impossibilities into possibilities. Today, in a world that denies God's existence and our need for Jesus' forgiveness and salvation, there are women who continue to bring the word of God to future generations. We pray for our godmothers, women catechists, Religious Sisters, female lay ministers, and spiritual directors. Like Sarah, these women are divinely selected and ordained as spiritual guides. Amen.

LET'S BE PERSISTENT

Mary Magdalene

As [Mary] wept, she bent over to look into the tomb; and she saw two angels in white, sitting where the body of Jesus had been lying ... They said to her, "Woman, why are you weeping?" She said to them, "They have taken away my Lord, and I do not know where they have laid him." When she had said this, she turned around and saw Jesus standing there, but she did not know that it was Jesus. Jesus said to her, "Woman, why are you weeping? For whom are you looking?" Supposing him to be the gardener, she said to him, "Sir, if you have carried him away, tell me where you have laid him, and I will take him away." Jesus said to her, "Mary!" She turned and said to him in Hebrew, "Rabbouni!" (which means Teacher). JOHN 20:11-16

PAUSE & REFLECT
Mary Magdalene: the Apostle to the Apostles, the patron saint of preachers. The woman who stood by Jesus, whose love for and faith in him never faltered. While others denied him and hid, she never doubted or ran away. Mary Magdalene: the faithful friend of Jesus who walked with him to the cross and rushed to his tomb to care for his dead body. Mary Magdalene: the first person to whom Jesus chose to reveal his resurrected body. Mary Magdalene: the brave woman who ran to the frightened men to proclaim the Good News. In a society in which women were powerless, you, Mary of Magdala, broke the chains of oppression.

HEAR OUR PRAYER...
We pray to you, St. Mary Magdalene, in thanksgiving for the brave women in our world today who have broken through the walls of a male-dominated society and patriarchal Church: women athletes, CEOs, government leaders, military personnel, chaplains and parish ministers, Vatican officials. Like Mary Magdalene, these women have been ridiculed, doubted, and denied. And, like Mary, they remain faithful and persistent; their actions and accomplishments proclaim to the world the strengths and gifts God has bestowed upon women. Amen.

LET'S TURN TO EACH OTHER

Elizabeth and Mary, the Mother of God

In those days Mary set out and went with haste to a Judean town in the hill country, where she entered the house of Zechariah and greeted Elizabeth. And Mary remained with her for about three months and then returned to her home. LUKE 1:39-40, 56

PAUSE & REFLECT

The young woman Mary traveled "with haste" to visit Elizabeth. Did Mary rush to her older relative to congratulate Elizabeth on the surprising news that Elizabeth was pregnant? Perhaps. But one wonders if that was Mary's sole motivation for making the journey and then staying with Elizabeth for three months. Mary, an unmarried pregnant teenager, confused and frightened, sought protection. While the angel told Mary not to be frightened, she needed the comfort and understanding of another woman, a woman with life experience. Elizabeth would know how to advise her; Elizabeth would protect her; Elizabeth would not condemn her.

And so it was. During those three months with Elizabeth, Mary worked through her fears, deepened her faith in and understanding of what the angel had spoken to her, and grew in self-confidence. After this time with Elizabeth, Mary, who was likely visibly pregnant, was strong enough to return to her family and town without yielding to their judgment. Mary had come to realize the gift she carried within her womb and had gained the strength to share the gift of the Messiah with the world.

Hear Our Prayer...

We pray for those women to whom we run, seeking advice and comfort: the women who will encourage and understand us; the women who challenge and protect us. We encounter these women in a variety of circumstances: they are our coaches, mentors, therapists, teachers, counselors, and older relatives. Like Elizabeth, through example and word, they provide us with an opportunity to grow in a deeper understanding of our God-given gifts and the strength and confidence to share those gifts. Amen.

LET'S KEEP OUR CHILDREN SAFE

Miriam

The daughter of Pharaoh came down to bathe at the river ... She saw the basket among the reeds and sent her maid to bring it. When she opened it, she saw the child. He was crying, and she took pity on him. "This must be one of the Hebrews' children," she said. Then his sister said to Pharaoh's daughter, "Shall I go and get you a nurse from the Hebrew women to nurse the child for you?" Pharaoh's daughter said to her, "Yes." So the girl went and called the child's mother.
EXODUS 2:4–8

Pause & Reflect

The young girl Miriam grew up during a time of violence, fear, and oppression against the Hebrew people. Moses' sister knew of Pharaoh's decree to kill all infant boys. And so, she courageously enacted a plan to save her brother's life. Miriam, a Hebrew child, dared to speak to Pharaoh's daughter, offering to help her with the infant. Imagine how their mother felt when Miriam called her to Pharaoh's daughter and heard the command to take her own son to nurse him! Not only did Miriam's plan save Moses, but it also kept her family together during the years that Moses grew. Unknowingly, Miriam set the stage for God's enslaved Chosen People to be freed.

HEAR OUR PRAYER...
We pray for the women who, like Miriam, courageously and selflessly protect all children who are in danger. We pray for women who work in health care professions: nurses, doctors, pharmacists, technicians, and therapists. We pray for all women who advocate for children: social workers, lawyers, police officers. We pray for older sisters, babysitters, and childcare workers. Like Miriam, during times of fear and violence, they often dare to speak and act to save a child's life, heal a family, and offer freedom from injustice. Amen.

LET'S WELCOME THE STRANGER

Rebecca

The children struggled together within her; and she said, "If it is to be this way, why do I live?" So she went to inquire of the Lord. And the Lord said to her, "Two nations are in your womb, and two peoples born of you shall be divided; one shall be stronger than the other; the elder shall serve the younger." **GENESIS 25:22-23**

Pause & Reflect

Rebecca—whose name means "to bind," "to tether," "to tie fast"—was a woman who endured much to ensure that the promise of the divine ancestral lineage would prosper. She had a painful and difficult pregnancy. The struggle that took place in her womb between her twin sons, Esau and Jacob, continued as they grew into manhood. While her husband, Isaac, favored the firstborn, Esau, Rebecca knew that he was not fit to become the Father of the Twelve Tribes. Rebecca risked being cursed by her husband and put into action a plan that would make Jacob the successor. By deceiving her dying husband, Rebecca intervened, and Isaac bestowed his blessing upon Jacob. Rebecca was a strong, forceful woman whose voice was listened to. She was determined that the lineage would continue with a woman from her homeland of Haran. So focused on this outcome was she that Rebecca exclaimed that if Jacob married a Canaanite woman, her life was of no value. Rebecca knew that only a strong, determined woman from Haran, a woman like herself, would bind the ancestral promise made to Abraham and Sarah.

Hear Our Prayer...

Like Rebecca, there are women today who speak out, who take risks, who place themselves in danger to provide for their children and their future generations. We pray especially for women throughout the world who seek asylum in foreign countries. Such women leave their homelands in search of safety, increased economic opportunities, and improved educational and healthcare systems—for their families and for themselves. We pray that our foremother Rebecca will watch

LET'S PUT OUR PRAYER INTO ACTION

Martha and Mary of Bethany

[Jesus] entered a certain village, where a woman named Martha welcomed him into her home. She had a sister named Mary, who sat at the Lord's feet and listened to what he was saying. But Martha was distracted by her many tasks; so she came to him and asked, "Lord, do you not care that my sister has left me to do all the work by myself? Tell her then to help me." LUKE 10:38-40

Now Bethany was near Jerusalem, some two miles away, and many of the Jews had come to Martha and Mary to console them about their brother. When Martha heard that Jesus was coming, she went and met him, while Mary stayed at home. JOHN 11:18-20

PAUSE & REFLECT

These two passages tell the story of both Martha and Mary; not of one or the other. These sisters' actions complement each other. While Mary chose to sit and listen to Jesus as Martha moved about and served, it was Martha who went to be with Jesus, leaving her sister at home mourning their dead brother. Neither sister's action or inaction is right or wrong; this is not a matter of either/or, but of both. Being with Jesus—praying—is not a matter of either being silent or taking action; prayer is both stillness and action. Prayer is a matter of both being and doing. Our quiet time with God will call us forth to action, and our action will lead us to reflect and pray. Prayers without action are empty words, and action without prayer is self-serving and reactionary.

HEAR OUR PRAYER...
We pray for women who exemplify how to live a life devoted to prayerful action: women such as Dorothy Day, co-founder of the Catholic Worker movement; St. Teresa of Calcutta, founder of the Missionaries of Charity; and Elizabeth Ann Seton, founder of the Catholic education system in the US. We pray for all women who devote their lives to hospitality, to motherhood, to education, and to health care. We pray with gratitude for all women who embody these words of St. (Mother) Teresa: "It's not how much we do but how much love we put into the doing." Amen.

LET'S CALL HER BLESSED

Mary, the Mother of God

The angel said to her, "Do not be afraid, Mary, for you have found favor with God. And now, you will conceive in your womb and bear a son, and you will name him Jesus." LUKE 1:30-31

And Mary said, "My soul magnifies the Lord, and my spirit rejoices in God my Savior, for he has looked with favor on the lowliness of his servant. Surely, from now on all generations will call me blessed."
LUKE 1:46-48

Pause & Reflect
Mary, chosen by God to be the mother of the Savior. A young virgin called upon to fulfill such a formidable mission. At the time of the annunciation, Mary could not have fully comprehended all that would unfold for her as the mother of Jesus. She watched him grow from a child into adulthood. She was by his side during his years of preaching and ministering, and she stood at his feet at his moment of death. How she must have experienced every human emotion during the lifetime of her son!

Hear Our Prayer...
We pray for all women. We pray for mothers and those women who love with a nurturing heart. We pray for women who rejoice with gratitude for all that God has done for them and for women who tremble with fear. We pray for women who sleep soundly at night in the comfort of their homes and for women who wander city streets in search of a safe place to rest their heads. We pray for women of all professions, races, and religions.

We pray:
Hail, Mary, full of grace, the Lord is with thee.
Blessed art thou among women and blessed is
    the fruit of thy womb, Jesus.
Holy Mary, Mother of God, pray for us sinners,
    now and at the hour of our death.
Amen.